THE LADY WHO COULDN'T SEE

CARY HOLBERT

ISBN-13: 978-0615890203
ISBN-10: 0615890202

Book cover by Joleene Naylor

Introduction

The Dirty Feet Ministries Bible Studies Series is designed to encourage you to reflect honestly on your life and then make adjustments to improve areas you identify as missing the mark of Jesus. The study is a collection of six actual events, with fictitious names given to the characters, followed by a Bible passage and then probing questions.

Dirty Feet Ministries believes the Word of God is the final rule for faith and life. In other words, all we need to know about God and to live for God is in the Bible. The real life events are given as examples of what life looks like when a person says yes to Jesus Christ and His will, or, in some cases, rebels against Him. The Word of God is given not just to read or develop a theology of words but to reveal God so that we might know Him and enjoy Him.

Those who have received mercy are destined to extend it to others. Mercy transcends physical limitations and has an eternal reach as an attribute of God. This study will examine how mercy of one who was blind conquered the blindness of one who was physically whole. Take this journey of mercy with us as we travel along side of one who could have grumbled and complained but instead marveled in the grace and mercy of God.

The Architect of the universe and Creator of all things is saying, Come to me and I will enable you to love, live, and enjoy life to the fullest. In our broken world, it is time for those who know God to fine-tune our lives for Him, and for those who don't, to turn to Him.

Table of Contents

The Event

Located in rural America, it was an older home, built in 1910 during the golden age of coal mining. The Robinson family had moved to the area years before, and were nobodies and outsiders in a small cliquish community. The house was located on Stony Street, a narrow street with cars always traveling too fast down it; it was an accident waiting to happen. Behind this home, there was a church that could seat about 500 people, which was relatively large for the area. Mr. Robinson was struggling, empty, and desperate; and floundering as a husband and father. He was even willing to give religion a shot if that would bring peace into his life and help him to be a good husband and father. It seemed pretty hopeless to him but out of desperation, he and his family attended the large upscale church.

The Robinsons noticed that one of their neighbors also attended the church. She appeared to be blind and it was both terrifying and fascinating to watch her walk down the sidewalk and then cross this narrow street that cars routinely used as a drag strip. This neighbor, Mrs. Hitt, had a cane and it was captivating to watch her navigate to the edge of the curb, patiently and gently probing her path. She must have had keen hearing because once she committed to crossing the street, she never hesitated. It seemed that she had also memorized the number of steps to cross because it was a light touch of the curb with her cane then one elevated step and she moved on to the church. Rain or shine she walked, and not just once but three times a week.

The father of four and husband, Mr. Robinson, had spent his life figuring things out the hard way and it had taken its toll on him. He was finally out of ideas and the light switch remained stuck in the off position. The phone rang one afternoon and it was the lady who couldn't see. She'd heard that the Robinsons were visiting the church where she was a member and she wanted to tell them how great it was to have them there and how important they were to the life of the church. She wanted them to know that they could call her if they needed anything. Mr. Robinson noticed something real about her care for his family. What was so amazing was the joy and hope she had even though she couldn't see. There was no resentment or complaints; just joy. There was a new member's class starting and the lady called to encourage them to join and so, out of respect for her, Mr. Robinson and his wife went to the class. The lady who couldn't see desperately wanted them to meet her friend, Jesus.

It was one of those God things as the new member's class started and Mr. Robinson came as one who couldn't see. During the class, the doom and gloom that had so gripped him was lifted and the scales that had been covering his eyes was removed. Finally, this wandering husband, who had been groping in the darkness, met the glorious Jesus. The lady who could not see had accomplished her mission for her friend, Jesus.

Not long after this event, Mrs. Hitt's husband, who was not blind, died. Mr. Robinson's daughters stayed a few nights with her, and Mr. Robinson helped repair one of her exterior doors. The lady who couldn't see saw more clearly than any person he knew. She could see well into the future and she knew all her infirmities would be healed when she met her friend Jesus.

Her race was coming to an end and she was now in

a nursing home with cancer. She had one final task and that was to brand deeply into Mr. Robinson's heart the confidence he needed to stay on course. Mr. Robinson made his way to the nursing home to see her and as he approached the threshold of the room, he saw she was staring at the ceiling, talking to Jesus, and he was confident that her earthly infirmity was gone. At that very moment, before he could say anything or announce himself, she said, "<u>Our friend</u> Mr. Robinson is here." She asked how he was doing and they prayed together and she went to see Jesus that day.

Lesson I

Who is blind?

If the Great Physician examined your life, what do you think His diagnosis would be concerning your spiritual life?

The event

1. Who had a better handle on life at the outset?

2. What impairment could have stopped Mrs. Hitt from working to improve the life of others?

3. Did Mrs. Hitt's life itself speak as well as her words?

4. Who was able to see beyond their present limitations clearly?

5. How would you describe Mr. Robinson's life initially?

The Bible Passage
John 9:1-41
Your current situation does not limit the work of God nor diminish the possibility of you being an instrument of God and influencing those around you.

1. John 9:1-41
    a. Who are the people in the plot?

2. John 9:11
    a. Who healed the man born blind?

3. John 9:35-38

   a. Was there a spiritual blindness that needed healing as well?

4. John 9:39-41

   a. What was the state of the Pharisees?

5. John 9:39-41

   a. What did the Pharisees need to do?

6. How would you describe your spiritual state?

Remember:

1. Our greatest need is to be spiritually healed and reconciled to God.

2. Self-righteousness is an impediment to Spiritual healing.

Lesson II

Who is your best friend?

Who do you spend time with in your life? Take just one day and journal your day's activities. Then examine the day's events and see how much time you spent with Jesus.

The Event

1. How would you describe the relationship between Jesus and Mrs. Hitt?

2. In what way did Mrs. Hitt demonstrate that Jesus was her friend?

3. Who was in Mrs. Hitt's circle of friends?

4. Who's your best friend?

5. What kind of friend are you?

The Bible Passage
John 15:9-17
The time spent cultivating a relationship has a direct bearing on the outcome.

1. John 15:9

   a. How is the relationship described between Jesus and His Father?

2. John 15:10-11

   a. How does a person demonstrate his love for

Jesus?

3. John 15:12-13

   a. How does Jesus demonstrate love for His friends?

4. John 15:14-15

   a. How does Jesus refer to those who trust in Him?

5. John 15:16-17

   a. How did we end up a friend of Jesus?

Remember:

   1. Jesus has demonstrated His love for us by dying in our place and paying the penalty for our sins and now calls those who trust in Him, friends. We need to make our friend Jesus our top priority in our many relationships

Lesson III

I can't wait to introduce you.

Who is the last person you introduced to Jesus?

The Event

1. If someone asked Mrs. Hitt who is the most important person in the world, who do you think she would choose?

2. Who do you think Mrs. Hitt was going to introduce next to Jesus?

3. In what ways did Mrs. Hitt introduce or make possible for Mr. Robinson to meet Jesus?

4. Do you have a top ten list of people you want to introduce to Jesus?

5. What was the result of Mr. Robinson being introduced to Jesus?

The Bible Passage
John 1:35-42
Your family and friends are only as important as Jesus is to you.

1. How important is your family to you?

2. John 1:35-40
    a. Who did Andrew follow?

3. John 1:38

   a. How does Andrew address Jesus?

4. John 1:41

   a. What is the first thing Andrew did after he committed to follow Jesus?

5. John 1:42

   a. What happened?

Remember:

   1. You need to develop a top ten list of people you plan to introduce to Jesus, and then do it.

Lesson IV

The team working together

What a privilege it is to be adopted into the family of God. We have new brothers and sisters who share a like mind and purpose. Are you using your talents and gifts in the team effort for the work of God?

The Event

1. If you attend a church, how does your team function to reach others?

2. What are some examples of how others were involved in reaching Mr. Robinson with the gospel?

3. Do you know your spiritual gift?

4. What do you think Mrs. Hitt's spiritual gift may have been?

5. What happens if you remove one of the key players from the event?

The Bible Passage
Hebrews 10:19-25
Our fellowship serves to fan the flame of our passions for Christ and His work.

1. Hebrews 10:19-23
   a. Why is the church to be one body?

2. Hebrews 10:24

   a. How would you describe our responsibility to one another?

3. Hebrews 10:24

   a. What happens when people encourage one another?

4. Hebrews 10:25

   a. What is expected of a team member?

5. Hebrews 10:25

   a. Why should we be motivated to work together and reach people who don't know Jesus?

Remember:

1. You need to be a member of a local church.

2. You need to discover and put to use your spiritual gift(s).

3. You need to work as a team member, not an ego maniac.

Lesson V

Reaping what you sow

Are you investing in the work of the Kingdom of God with your talents, treasure, and time, or in yourself?

The Event

1. What happened to Mrs. Hitt's husband?

2. Can you imagine being blind and living alone after losing your spouse who could see? How did this impact everyday living?

3. What had Mrs. Hitt been sowing?

4. She was at church regularly and caring for those outside of the church so do you think she was alone?

5. Who was Mrs. Hitt's friend while she was on her death bed?

The Bible Passage
Galatians 6:7-9
Who directs the use of all your resources?

1. Galatians 6:7
    a. What do you harvest?

2. Galatians 6:8

a. What happens to self-centered people?

3. Galatians 6:8
   a. What does it mean to please the Spirit?

4. Galatians 6:9
   a. What are we never to get tired of doing?

5. Galatians 6:9
   a. When do we reap our harvest?

Remember:

1. God is to direct the use of your time, talents, and treasures.

2. You will give an account to God on how you utilized your time, talents, and treasures.

Lesson VI

Full circle

It is rare to find people who are faithful from the beginning to the end. The lady started out faithful and ended faithful. How about you?

The Event

1. How did the journey begin between Mrs. Hitt and her new neighbors, the Robinsons?

2. In the end, who was the teacher and who the pupil?

3. How consistent are you in living for Christ?

4. In the end, how did her cancer-ridden body impact her witness for Jesus?

5. Why do you think Mrs. Hitt's life was such a powerful witness to this man and his family?

The Bible Passage
2 Timothy 4:1-8
Rest in what Christ alone has done and stay on His course, no matter how tough the going gets. Endure to the end. Keep the Faith!

1. 2 Timothy 4:1-2
    a. What was Timothy continually to do, no matter what the circumstances?

2. 2 Timothy 4:3-4

    a. How will some people respond to the Word of God?

3. 2 Timothy 4:5

    a. What is something that can impede Timothy's ministry?

4. 2 Timothy 4:6

    a. How did the reality of death impact Paul's ministry?

5. 2 Timothy 4:7-8

    a. What is the one attribute Paul used to describe his life from the time he met Jesus?

Remember:

1. We can expect obstacles, disappointments, and trials of many kinds as Christians but we are to be faithful throughout those events.

2. Our fears at times attempt to derail our faithful journey so we have to rise above them.

Lesson VII

Mission accomplished

You will always be remembered for how you finish. Finish well!

The Event

1. Can you say, if you died today, that you have accomplished all that God desired of you?

2. Do you think Mrs. Hitt, who couldn't physically see, finished all that God had desired of her? Why or Why not?

3. How well did Mrs. Hitt finish?

4. How do you think her hope of the future impacted her living?

5. If you had to rank prayer as an important component of Mrs. Hitt's life between 1 and 10, with 10 meaning very important, what would it be? Why?

The Bible Passage
Matthew 25:31-46
Are you one who walks by someone in need or are you the one who stops and helps? Those who have received mercy are destined to extend it to others.

1. Matthew 25:31-32
    a. What will happen when time as we know it comes to an end?

2. Matthew 25:33

    a. What names are given to the two groups of people?

3. Matthew 25:37

    a. The ones on the right are called _____ ones. Why?

4. Matthew 25:34-40

    a. How is the life of the sheep described and how does it end?

5. Matthew 25:41-46

    a. How is the life of the goat described and how does it end?

Remember:

1. You will always be remembered by how you finish.

Lesson VIII

What now?

Many folks will finish what they're doing, wash their hands then move on to the next life event. This pattern repeats itself in the Christian community as well. You spend six to eight weeks reading, fellowshipping, praying, and completing exercises only to move on to the next event in your life. Often our faith is not more than an inch deep and nothing more than hot air. We are robbed and rob others of all that God wants for humanity.

Mrs. Hitt, who was blind, read Braille and talked to the Lord, refuses to just move on to the next event. For her to live was Jesus Christ. It was a way of life, not a compartment of life. Who can you name that you personally introduced to Jesus Christ? This call to make Christ known is for all who are part of the body of Christ. Just think how many people and generations will be impacted for eternity because of Mrs. Hitt's life. When you are finishing your race, what will your life have amounted to for eternity, because everything else you will leave behind.

Author Biography

Cary Holbert is a pastor, public speaker, author, and financial and management advocate. As a public speaker, Pastor Cary has specialized in vision casting for over 25 years. Pastor Cary has successfully helped both non-profit and for-profit organizations in financial and management aspects of their business. With a Master's degree in Pastoral Leadership from the Columbia Biblical Seminary, Pastor Cary serves on the board of the Garden Worship Center and is also the President of the Dirty Feet Ministries, which writes and publishes ministry training literature, including *The Elder Handbook, Part I & II,* and *The Dirty Feet Ministries Small Group Bible Study Six Part Series.*

Books by Dirty Feet Ministries, Inc

Small Group Bible Study:

The Lady Who Couldn't See
I'm Too Old
The Dad Who Left Me
Why Give Money?
I've Tried Everything, Except
Who is Your Timothy or Lydia?

Leadership Training:

The Elder
The Elder in Action
The Deacon

The Servant Series:

1 Peter

Our Website:
http://www.christianbooksbible.org/

Our email:
christianbiblebooks@sc.rr.com